Manchester United

Peter Leigh

Published in association with The Basic Skills Agency

Hodder & Stoughton

Acknowledgements
Photos: pp. iv, 9, 17 © Colorsport.
pp. 5, 22, 25, 26 © Action Images.
p. 14 © MSI.
Cover photo: © MSI.

Orders: please contact Bookpoint Ltd, 130 Milton Park, Abingdon, Oxon OX14 4SB. Telephone: (44) 01235 827720. Fax: (44) 01235 400454. Lines are open from 9.00–6.00, Monday to Saturday, with a 24-hour message answering service. Email address: orders@bookpoint.co.uk

British Library Cataloguing in Publication Data
A catalogue record for this title is available from The British Library

ISBN 0 340 70102 1

First published 1997
Impression number   10 9 8 7 6 5
Year   2005 2004 2003 2002 2001

Typeset by Fakenham Photosetting Ltd, Fakenham, Norfolk,
Printed in Great Britain for Hodder & Stoughton Educational, a division of Hodder Headline Plc,
338 Euston Road, London NW1 3BH by The Bath Press, Bath

Contents

Matt Busby and the Busby Babes.
FA Cup Final. Manchester v Aston Villa, 1957.

1 The Busby Babes

The sky was grey.
Snow covered the airport.

The plane was waiting on the runway.
There was snow on the runway
but it was starting to melt
and turn to slush.
More snow was coming.

The captain looked through the windscreen,
and thought about taking off.

He had already tried twice.
Both times he had failed.

The big plane was full.
On board were sports writers, photographers
and football fans.
And there was also
the most famous football team in the world.

Manchester United!

Everybody was talking about them.
They were so young and full of life.
They had already won the League twice.
Many of them were teenagers,
and the captain was only 28.

That's why they were called the Busby Babes,
after their Scottish manager Matt Busby.
They were all star players:
Tommy Taylor, Duncan Edwards,
and especially the new star, Bobby Charlton.

Bobby Charlton had scored two goals
in the match that day.
They had beaten Red Star Belgrade,
and were now in the semi-final
of the European Cup.
That was Matt Busby's dream,
to win the European Cup.
If they did,
they would be the first British club
ever to win it.

The captain looked at the runway again.
Perhaps he shouldn't try again.
But he had only stopped for more fuel.
The team was tired
and keen to get home.
They had another important match
on Saturday.

The sports writers were keen to get home too.
They had to write their stories for the papers.

And the fans were keen to get home,
so they could tell everybody about the game.

The captain eased the plane onto the runway.
He would try once more.

The plane roared along the runway.
The tail-lights disappeared
into the snow and darkness.

But the plane never took off.

The snow and slush slowed the plane down
so it couldn't take off.
It skidded off the runway
and smashed through the fence.
It crashed into a house,
and burst into flames.

Twenty three people died,
including eight Manchester United players.

The Busby Babes were no more.

That was 6 February 1958,
the darkest day in the history
of Manchester United.
The day of the Munich air crash.

The darkest day in the history of Manchester United.
The Munich air crash, 6 February 1958.

When the news reached England
people cried in the streets.
They gathered round the radio or television
listening to the list of dead and injured.

Matt Busby was the worst injured.
For months he couldn't move.
When he finally went back to Manchester,
thousands of people cheered him
in the streets.

They felt sorry for him.
They thought he was brave,
but they thought he was finished.

They were wrong!

While he was in hospital
for all those months
Matt Busby had decided to start again.
He would build another Manchester United,
a second Busby Babes.
And they would be even better than the first.
And this time they would win
the European championship!

2 The New Babes

Matt Busby built his new team
round the players who had survived
the Munich air crash,
especially Bobby Charlton.

Bobby Charlton was a wonderful player.
He had a swerve
that could fool a whole team,
and a left-foot shot that could score goals
from 40 metres.
His brother Jack was also a footballer.

Soon Manchester United began to win again.
They were even in the Cup Final
the same year as Munich!

In 1962, Matt Busby brought Denis Law
to Old Trafford,
the Manchester United home ground.
He was Scottish,
but had been playing in Italy.
He had a shock of blond hair
and was razor-sharp near goal.

Denis Law started to score
and in 1963 they won the FA Cup.
Everyone was talking about
Bobby Charlton and Denis Law.

But then in 1963,
a slim, black-haired, young Irishman
played his first game for Manchester United.
Soon he would be more famous
than even Bobby Charlton and Denis Law.
Soon he would be the greatest player
in English football,
and (some say) in the world.
He was George Best.

The magic of George Best.
Manchester United v Crystal Palace, 1971.

3 George Best

There was a magic about George Best.

Millions of people watched Manchester United
just to see George Best.
And they still remember
the games he played in
and the things he did.
Because the things he did seemed impossible.
You could not believe
what you were seeing.

He would twist and turn,
left and right,
backwards and forwards.
The ball seemed stuck to his feet.
He would go round defenders,
between defenders,
and through defenders.

He would be in the corner of the field,
with three defenders around him.
Suddenly he would be past them,
with his shirt outside his shorts,
and the ball still at his feet.
The defenders were left standing there,
looking at each other,
feeling silly.

How did he do that?
Nobody could do that!
George Best could!

Or he would play the ball
off the legs of the defenders.
You thought it was just luck,
until he did it again!
And again!

Then he would shoot from a crazy position,
and the ball would swerve into the net.

It was impossible!
Nobody could score like that!
But George Best did!

The crowd would watch
with their mouths open.
They could not believe
what they had just seen.
And then the roars and shouts and claps
would roll round the ground.
George Best had done it again.

What made him so good?

He was small.
He looked thin and weak.
But he wasn't.
He was wiry
and much stronger than he looked.

He was nimble and very quick,
and always kept his eyes on the ball,
just in front of his toes.
He never even seemed to look up.

But perhaps you can't explain it.
Perhaps it was just genius!

But he wasn't just a football star.

He was more like a pop star,
or a film star.

He drove fast cars,
and had famous girlfriends.
He threw all-night parties at expensive clubs.
His picture was always in the papers,
or in the magazines,
or on the television.
Girls screamed when he ran on the pitch.
They mobbed his car,
and camped outside his house.

He was the first football superstar!

4 Europe

Manchester United were again
the best team in England.
They won the Cup once
and the League twice.
And then in 1968
they got to the final of the European Cup.

It was just ten years after Munich,
ten years after the death of the Busby Babes.

Everyone knew
what this match
meant for Matt Busby.

Bobby Charlton said afterwards:
'It was our duty.
It had become a family thing.'
He had been at Munich too.

The final was at Wembley.
It was against Benfica.
It was a tight, hard game.
United were leading 1–nil
for most of the game.
Then Benfica equalised
in the last few minutes.
It would be extra time.

The United players sat down
in the centre of the pitch.
They looked tired out.
Matt Busby moved quietly among them,
talking to each one,
trying to inspire them,
to urge them on.

United started extra time like a new team.
Best tore through the defence,
swerved round the goalkeeper
and clipped the ball
into the back of the net.

2–1!

Then Brian Kidd made it 3–1,
and finally Charlton scored the fourth.

4–1!

Manchester United had won.
They had won the European Cup.
At last.
As the team collected the cup,
some people said
they saw others among the team.
The spirits of the Busby Babes!

The country went wild.
George Best was voted
Footballer of the Year,
then Player of the Year.
There was a message from the Queen.
Matt Busby was now Sir Matt Busby!

George Best holding the Cup he helped to win.
European victory against Benfica, 1968.

A dream come true.
Matt Busby with the European Cup, 1968.

5 Dark days

Winning the European Cup
was the high point for Manchester United.
Everything seemed to go downhill from then on.
Sir Matt Busby retired.
He stayed with the club,
but not as manager.

Lots of new managers were tried,
but none of them settled.

It was hard to follow Sir Matt Busby.

Some of the older players were past their best.
Denis Law was transferred.
In 1974, Bobby Charlton played his last game.

But the worst problem was George Best.
There was too much pressure on him.
He had a drink problem.
He started missing training,
and even missing matches.

In 1972, George Best left Manchester United
and hardly ever played again.

He was only 26!

These were dark days for United.
But the worst came in 1974.
They had slipped down the league table
and then they were relegated!

It sent a huge shock through all football.
How could Manchester United be sent down?
They bounced back straightaway,
and went back up in 1975,
but they were not the same United.

They did have some success
in the next few years,
but they didn't really settle until 1986.
In that year
the team got a new manager,
Alex Ferguson.

6 The Team Today

Alex Ferguson was Scottish
like Matt Busby.
He started to build a team
around the captain, Bryan Robson.
Bryan was a great player.
He was also captain of England,
but he had a terrible injury to his shoulder,
which stopped him playing at his best.

Alex brought in other players
like Mark Hughes and Paul Ince,
and foreign players
like Andrei Kanchelskis
and the goal keeper Peter Schmeichel.

He has also brought on young players
like Ryan Giggs.
People call Ryan the new George Best.
He's just as popular with the fans
especially the girls!

Alex Ferguson holding the FA Cup
and the Premier League Trophy, 1996.

The new Manchester United
is even more successful
than the great teams of the past.
They have won the League and Cup,
and the Double twice!
No other club has done that.

Perhaps their most famous player today
is Eric Cantona.
But for not all the right reasons.
He can be moody and difficult.

In 1994 he was sent off.
As he was going
a man in the crowd shouted something at him.

Eric went mad.
He ran and kicked at the man
Then he was hurried off the field.

Millions of people saw Cantona's kick
on television.
There were arguments about it
for days afterwards.
The papers went on and on about it,
the television showed it time and time again.
There were even arguments about it
in Parliament.
Should Cantona be charged?
Should he be fined,
or imprisoned?
Should he be sent back to France?

In the end,
Cantona was given Community Service,
and suspended from football.

Two of the most famous players of 1996.
Ryan Giggs and Eric Cantona.

It was a hard blow
for someone as proud as Eric.
But when he returned to Manchester United
he seemed better.
He was calmer,
and more in control of himself.

You could see this
in the Cup Final in 1996.

With nearly the last kick of the game,
Eric calmly scored the goal
that won the Cup for Manchester.

The winning team.
Manchester United in 1996.

7 Sir Matt Busby

It was a cold, grey day in Manchester.
The shops had closed early.
The traffic had stopped.
The streets were full but quiet.
The people were standing in silence
as a funeral passed slowly by them.
It was the funeral of Sir Matt Busby.

All the old players were there,
including George Best and Bobby Charlton,
(now Sir Bobby Charlton).
Standing with them were the new players
like Ryan Giggs and Eric Cantona.

They were standing in respect
for one of the great names of football,
Sir Matt Busby.
And the club that will always be linked to that
name,
Manchester United!